The
Capitalist
Manifesto

The
Capitalist
Manifesto

The End of Class Warfare,
Toward Universal Affluence

Ralph Benko and William R. Collier, Jr.

THE WEBSTERS' PRESS
Washington, DC, 2019

CONTENTS

"It is the great multiplication of the productions of all the different arts, in consequence of the division of labour, which occasions, in a well-governed society, that universal opulence which extends itself to the lowest ranks of the people."

— *Adam Smith, An Inquiry into the Nature and Causes of the Wealth of Nations*

FOREWORD

I am proud to be both a product and a producer of the "Supply-Side Revolution." *Wealth and Poverty*, my worldwide best seller, was called a "manifesto" for capitalism and made me Ronald Reagan's most quoted living author.

At the time, America confronted a so-called Misery Index spiking as high as 20%. America was suffering, at the time, from simultaneous 10% inflation and 10% unemployment. That was deemed an impossibility by the Keynesian and socialist-leaning Establishment.

But there it was, intractable and baffling to the political elites of the day as so-called "negative interest rates" confound the economists of today.

Ronald Reagan, adopted our proposed radical change of policy. Mocked by many as "voodoo economics," it ushered in a new era of prosperity. On the day Reagan declared for the presidency in November 1979 the Dow was at 814. At the time of this writing it is now over 27,000.

What caused this almost unimaginable growth in national wealth?

Capitalism.

Scores of other nations followed Reagan's free enterprise policy mix of lower marginal tax rates and stable measuring-stick money rather than "easy" money.

The most notable success story after the United States was in the People's Republic of China, which began by restoring stable money through a return to a gold standard and ultimately pegged its currency to the dollar.

As a matter of saving face, the Chinese leadership, declaring "to be rich is glorious," did not call it "capitalism." I call it the "information theory of economics" and the Chinese are now publishing all my books on the subject. But as the Chinese say, "whether the cat is black or white, what matters is whether it catches mice."

The enterprising Chinese took to free enterprise with gusto. China led the human race's worldwide annual income growth from $11T to over $83T. According to *time-prices* that measure the value of goods and services by the number of hours of work it takes to earn them, the Chinese government has actually underestimated its rate of innovation and growth.

Amid many conflicting signals, the Chinese appear ready to continue their success propelled by private sector entrepreneurship in "free zones", venture capital, and technological innovation.

Now, however, a new infatuation with socialism is emerging. Polls show that a majority of idealistic, though historically uninformed, youth register as sentimentally favorable toward socialism. In reaction, many conservatives are generating galaxies of pixels pointing out socialism's unbroken track record of failure.

The best defense against this potentially pernicious silliness of a resurgence of socialism is a good offense. Thus I enthusiastically welcome *The Capitalist Manifesto* and its affirmative celebration of capitalism.

It proclaims, as I did in <u>*Wealth and Poverty*</u>, the virtues of free enterprise. It does so with such simplicity and clarity that it rescues economics from its status as "the dismal science." *The Capitalist Manifesto* nicely complements my own paradigm-shifting theory of capitalism in <u>*Knowledge and Power*</u>, wherein I wrote:

> *Many free market advocates view capitalism as a system as dominated by incentives, with economic agents treated as inhabitants of a Skinner box driven by rewards and punishments.*
>
> *But, in fact, capitalism is an information and learning system governed by information as entrepreneurial surprise.*
>
> *Wealth is knowledge; growth is learning; money is real and reflects the abiding scarcity of time.*
>
> *The source of all progress is human creativity, which always comes as a surprise to us, joining information and enterprise."*
>
> *A critical moment in the development of my information theory of capitalism came when I read an essay by Princeton economist Albert Hirschman on the success or failure of UN development projects.*
>
> *The key was not good plans or available resources or virtuous developers. What differentiated successful from unsuccessful projects was entrepreneurial creativity.*
>
> *"Creativity," he wrote, "always comes as a surprise to us. If it didn't we wouldn't need it. And planning would work."*
>
> *As I added later, if creativity could be planned—if it were not surprising—socialism would work!*

> *I concluded that if information can be measured as surprise and entrepreneurial creativity could be measured as surprise, I could link the two together in an information theory of capitalism.*
>
> *I concluded that capitalism is not chiefly an incentive system, driven by rewards and punishments, by greed and desire.*
>
> *It is an information system, driven by curiosity and imagination, experiment and learning.*

Capitalism is not the tawdry thing that socialists label and libel it. Capitalism draws on the highest and best human qualities. Socialism, by contrast, represents nothing but an epic failure of the imagination of its proponents.

Benko and Collier dispel the canard that capitalism is excellent for generating wealth but terrible at equitably distributing it. They use as an epigram and a recurring theme Adam Smith's too often overlooked observation as to how capitalism, "in a well-governed society, [brings] that universal opulence which extends itself to the lowest ranks of the people."

This book provides an inspirational text for true capitalists, creative entrepreneurs. It is in itself an entrepreneurial surprise, responding to the needs of the world during a time of intellectual confusion.

The Capitalist Manifesto contributes to the new wealth of nations. The authors, and I, invite you to become full partners on the exciting new and ever expanding frontiers of true capitalism. In the words of Benko and Collier, capitalism "by its very nature is uniquely able to capture the adventure of discovery. Capitalism enables abundant new sources of wealth to be discovered and curated for the benefit of all people and the planet itself."

Join the information revolution on the frontiers of discovery.

George Gilder
The Berkshires
November 18, 2019

INTRODUCTION

True Capitalism is an economic system designed, in the words of Adam Smith, to bring about "universal opulence which extends itself to the lowest ranks of the people."

True Capitalism accomplishes this by rewarding valuable contributions to the general welfare. And, notwithstanding its persistent and even virulent criticisms from the left, true Capitalism has been proven to achieve its goal better than any other system.

In the immortal words of President John F. Kennedy in his last public speech, "A rising tide lifts all boats." Other systems, such as Socialism and its virulent form, Communism, have repeatedly claimed and repeatedly failed to achieve the goal of universal opulence.

Capitalism has allowed billions of people to rise from abject poverty and, by their own honest efforts, rise to economic security and even affluence. In addition to reasonable prosperity, true Capitalism thereby also offers agency and dignity.

By contrast, Socialism and Communism in practice have proved to be mere disguised and mechanized forms of Feudalism. Feudalism rewards people based on their status rather than their merit and service to the general welfare.

And yet, Capitalism's reputation is coming under renewed assault. The prestige of Socialism and Communism, which had been discredited by their many failures, is resurgent in the public discourse and mass media.

What's going on?

First, Capitalism has been consistently slandered both by its enemies and by successful capitalists who, having achieved the heights of opulence, now seek special status and privileges for themselves. Communists, since Marx and Engel's small Manifesto, have claimed that while Capitalism is unrivaled for creating wealth it is inferior in distributing wealth equitably in proportion to one's contribution to society.

Communists, ironically considering Communism's repeated failure to serve the interest of workers, consistently ignore that historical track record of true Capitalism. True Capitalism, while imperfect, has a vastly better track record of giving workers, and even the poor, the ways and means to rise to economic security and even affluence. Capitalism repeatedly has provided those means better than any other system ever tried.

Second, true Capitalism's enemies have had some success in conflating it with its opposite, cronyism. Capitalism, which demands equal opportunity for all, is the very opposite of cronyism. Socialism is the very embodiment of cronyism. Under Socialism the self-anointed, self-perpetuating, political elites allocate the nation's wealth to their favored recipients. In theory they will allocate equitably. In practice they have always been guilty of favoritism and, ultimately, cronyism.

Third, true Capitalism by its very nature is uniquely able to capture the adventure of discovery. True Capitalism uniquely respects human creativity, allowing abundant new sources of wealth to be discovered and curated for the benefit of all people and the planet itself.

Finally, Capitalists have been far too modest in their claims about Capitalism. One of liberty's greatest apostles, Friedrich Hayek, called for the creation of a utopian liberal (as in liberty!) movement. He prescribed this to capture the imagination of the people, especially the youth.

Only by appealing to the imagination, of a world of universal and equitable prosperity, will we be able to mobilize the masses to eradicate the last vestiges of Socialism (a form, as we shall see, of Feudalism) that make economic misery and humiliation persist.

Only by propounding the Capitalist Utopia will we be able to bring into being the Golden Age of prosperity, human dignity, world peace and ecology which only Capitalism can provide.

True Capitalism alone has proven itself, in practice, capable of bringing hundreds of millions and even billions out of abject poverty.

True Capitalism alone has proven itself capable of imbuing workers with agency and dignity.

True Capitalism, alone, has shown itself to have the power of bringing about the Utopia of which Socialists can only dream.

The Capitalist Manifesto's purpose is to spark just such a movement. We invite, indeed urge, you to support and even help lead such a movement.

EXECUTIVE SUMMARY

The Undead – Socialism – arises by night from its box of native soil.

There has been a recent resurgence in the popularity of Socialism. At least this appears to be so in the public conversation and in public opinion polls.

This apparent popularity is a reaction to abuses of Capitalism, not Capitalism. Capitalism is being blamed for leading people toward, and even into, penury. Untrue.

True Capitalism is not the perpetrator of economic or ecological injustice. The true culprit is favoritism and even Feudalism under a façade of Capitalism.

The indictment of Capitalism is understandable. It is also deeply misguided.

PART 1

CAPITALISM AND ITS ENEMIES

CAPITALISM

What is Capitalism?

To understand true Capitalism you have to start with an understanding of capital. Capital is the secret sauce of Capitalism. So, what is it?

The *New Oxford American Dictionary* defines capital as: wealth in the form of money or other assets owned by a person or organization or available or contributed for a particular purpose such as starting a company or investing…

- the excess of a company's assets over its liabilities.
- people who possess wealth and use it to control a society's economic activity, considered collectively…
- [with modifier] a valuable resource of a particular kind: *there is insufficient investment in human capital.*

In plain words, capital means tools and know-how. There's nothing sinister about it.

Skilled workers contribute more value and thus make more money than the semi-skilled. The semi-skilled contribute more and make more than the unskilled. Great tools make workers far more productive than crude tools. Crude tools make us more productive than no tools.

Capital is simply skills and tools.

Stocks and bonds are the classical instruments of Capitalism. These are "claim checks." They are the instruments proving that someone with savings has put those savings into a business, thereby owning a portion or being its lender.

The business then uses that money to build factories, warehouses, office space, or to buy equipment or other necessities for being productive. That's called "the cost of doing business."

People with know-how – the "human capital" – invent, build, sell, and distribute goods and services. These enterprises contribute more to the general welfare than they cost. That's "profit."

Profit is not a dirty word. If a business doesn't add more to the general welfare than its cost of doing business it doesn't last long. Ecologists are not the only ones concerned with sustainability.

True Capitalism rewards those who bring capital – skills and tools – to society. The more value they create for the rest of us the more profit they make. If profits get too high, competitors swoop in. Competition – not officious meddling – is what pushes prices down.

CAPITALISM HAS TWO ENEMIES.

The first mortal enemy of Capitalism is philosophical and obvious: Socialists, including those of its most virulent form, Communists, are committed to Capitalism's destruction and are forthright in declaring that.

The second mortal enemy is practical and unexpected: many successful Capitalists disdain, sometimes with implacable hostility, the system by which they achieved wealth.

The great classical liberal prophet and free market champion Friedrich Hayek wrote, in an essay titled *Intellectuals and Socialism* published in the Spring 1949 issue of *The University of Chicago Law Review*:

> The difficulty of finding genuine and disinterested support for a systematic policy for freedom is not new. In a passage of which the reception of a recent book of mine has often reminded me, Lord Acton long ago described how
>
> "At all times sincere friends of freedom have been rare, and its triumphs have been due to minorities, that have prevailed by associating themselves with auxiliaries whose objects differed from their own; and this association, which is always dangerous, has been sometimes disastrous, by giving to opponents just grounds of opposition…"
>
> More recently, one of the most distinguished living American economists has complained in a similar vein that the main task of those who believe in the basic principles of the capitalist system must frequently be to defend this system against the capitalists — indeed the great liberal economists, from Adam Smith to the present, have always known this.

. . .

> It may be that as a free society as we have known it carries in itself the forces of its own destruction, that once freedom has been achieved it is taken for granted and ceases to be valued, and that the free growth of ideas which is the essence of a free society will bring about the destruction of the foundations on which it depends.
>
> There can be little doubt that in countries like the United States the ideal of freedom today has less real appeal for the young than it has in countries where they have learned what its loss means.

Big Business today is often in cahoots with Big Government. Together they preserve the façade while hollowing out the substance of true Capitalism. Thus they enhance their privileges at our expense, traducing the soul of Capitalism.

Thus do some Capitalists seek to appropriate and devalue the Capitalist brand. Fat Cats are discrediting a fine philosophy.

They betray its essence to justify what are essentially feudalistic practices, economic success based on status rather than merit. By misappropriating and misrepresenting the Capitalist brand they persuade a naïve public to kill the goose that lays the golden eggs.

True Capitalism is an imperfect but, in practice, unrivaled mechanism to generate equitable prosperity. To reiterate the words of its original philosopher and prophet, Adam Smith, true Capitalism will produce "universal opulence which extends itself to the lowest ranks of the people."

True Capitalism is by nature equitable. Equitable is a fairer, more nuanced description for what is morally desirable than "equal."

Equality implies an undifferentiated sameness. A demand for equality of outcomes disregards legitimate differences.

Yes, assuredly, invidious discrimination is evil. And yet to call someone discriminating is a compliment. Discrimination based on legitimate factors makes one discriminating, not discriminatory.

Discriminatory means based on prejudice, an invidious quality.

This distinction makes all the difference.

EQUITY

Equity recognizes that – even with equality of opportunity – we'll enjoy different outcomes. Some will get richer.

That could be either right or wrong.

It is perfectly legitimate that those with greater talents, skills, and diligence – and who use their God-given gifts to make thousands, millions, even billions of people better off – become millionaires. Billionaires, even.

If someone creates trillions of dollars in value for others it is silly to begrudge her financial gain. No matter how large, it may well be a tiny fraction of the value she created for others. She won't be able to spend even a fraction of the wealth inuring to her no matter how hard she tries.

And she is far more likely to be a better steward of the abundance she created than any Congressperson, Senator... or even president. She has shown herself to have what one former president called "the money touch." Many politicians lack this skill.

Of course, luck plays its part in success. On the cover of *The Capitalist Manifesto* is a portrayal of the goddess Fortuna, the goddess of fortune and the "personification of luck." Lady Luck, like Lady Justice, is often portrayed as blindfolded.

Enjoying a lucky break does not carry with it the stigma associated with privilege. Some people will succeed through blind luck, not talent or virtue. That said, statistically speaking, luck is neutral.

Few begrudge the winner of the lottery. Fewer still begrudge whoever who heroically invented and delivered some new product or service that improves lives. Making room for luck, as true Capitalism does, is a small price to pay for its unrivaled power to create universal opulence extending even to the lowest order.

Honoring chance by no means justifies the successful Capitalist who proceeds to load the dice against other players. Rigging the game is antithetical to true Capitalism.

If your prosperity comes exclusively from status, such as celebrity, rather than merit, we hold that to be illegitimate. But hey, that's Feudalism for you. The favorable reception which Socialism now is beginning to receive reflects a just disgust for something masquerading as Capitalism. Not disgust for true Capitalism.

Pervasive privilege, sometimes called cronyism, is a mere caricature of Capitalism. Privilege bases itself on power, social rank, and connections. Status-based, it's a form of Feudalism. We also contend that Socialism, with its claims "so various, so beautiful, so new" is also but a species of Feudalism.

Socialism assigns exalted privileges – in society and in the economy – based on status. Marx and Engels, in *The Communist Manifesto*, identified the then-beneficiaries of such privilege as "the physician, the lawyer, the priest, the poet, the man of science." They invested these with the "halo." *The Communist Manifesto* describe them as "honored and looked up to with reverent awe."

Today we would add to the list of the privileged: socially exalted academics and politicos. These are the new aristocrats.

Capitalism rejects aristocracy. Capitalism strips the social status- based halo from all. True Capitalism honors those who make real contributions to equitable prosperity and the general welfare.

Feudalism doles out privileges as a function of elite status. Socialism, a form of Feudalism, is night to Capitalism's day.

PRIVILEGE AND PREJUDICE

The Communist Manifesto portrayed Capitalism as heading for the ash heap of history. It argued that Capitalism had vanquished Feudalism and brought about a new form of social injustice. In that unjust new order, the middle class, called the bourgeoisie, oppressed the working class, called the proletariat.

It argued that Communism would now supplant Capitalism and, it claimed, create a classless (and equal) society. Marx and Engels were right about Capitalism having vanquished Feudalism. History, however, proved them utterly wrong about Communism, of which Socialism is a milder form, bringing about a classless society. Class warfare instead brought penury and misery.

Many shed their blood in Communist revolutions, advancing or resisting them. In practice Communism revealed itself as a throwback to Feudalism. Socialism proved, in the words of Hayek, "the road to serfdom."

The ghost of Capitalism Past vanquished Feudalism. The ghost of "Capitalism" Present is infested with privilege. It is a monster that uses the rhetoric of free markets to defend special privileges. That's not true Capitalism. Overlooking the infection has tarnished the Capitalist brand.

GenX's, Millennials and GenZ's reject privileging the wealthy and powerful. Rightly so. They reject prejudicing students and workers. They are right to do so. They sense that something is not right. Rightly so.

Privilege is antithetical to true Capitalism.

Enter the spirit of Capitalism Future. True Capitalism rejects both privilege and prejudice. Those are artifacts of Feudalism, which invests its elites with privilege and saddles those of inferior social status with prejudice.

The spirit of Capitalism Future – real Capitalism based on free markets – promises transformation for the general welfare. It promises dignity and prosperity.

Capitalism offers the Utopia of liberty and justice for all.

THE SUBVERSION OF CAPITALISM BY ITS MERCHANTS

True Capitalism is synonymous with free markets. Free markets mean economic (and social) systems predicated on contributions to the general welfare based on the organic initiative of the participants themselves.

Free markets prohibit the use of force, fraud, or coercion. They are organic, not an arbitrary synthetic order imposed from above. Free markets are the essence of what makes and keeps Capitalism ethical and beneficial.

Adam Smith was the founding philosopher and prophet of free markets.

As Hayek noted, Smith was not naïve to the dangers posed to free markets *by merchants*. As Smith observed, in *Wealth of Nations*, "People of the same trade seldom meet together, even for merriment and diversion, but the conversation ends in a conspiracy against the public, or in some contrivance to raise prices."

Smith then went on to say:

> The interest of the dealers, however, in any particular branch of trade or manufactures, is always in some respects different from, and even opposite to, that of the public. To widen the market and to narrow the competition, is always in the interest of the dealers. To widen the market may frequently be agreeable enough to the interest of the public; but to narrow the competition must always be against it, and can serve only to enable the dealers, by raising their profits above what they naturally would be, to levy, for their own benefit, an absurd tax upon the rest of their fellow-citizens.

9

The proposal of any new law or regulation of commerce which comes from this order ought always to be listened to with great precaution, and ought never to be adopted till after having been long and carefully examined, not only with the most scrupulous, but with the most suspicious attention. It comes from an order of men whose interest is never exactly the same with that of the public, who have generally an interest to deceive and even to oppress the public, and who accordingly have, upon many occasions, both deceived and oppressed it.

Enemies of Capitalism seize on this wry indictment by Smith himself of this distortion by merchants as a confession of Capitalism's amorality. That's a misreading. Smith's indictment is of the merchants pursuing selfish interests. Not of Capitalism.

SOCIAL INSURANCE IS NOT SOCIALISM

One common claim by both socialists and cronyists is that social insurance is socialism. On the one hand it is meant to "prove" that if you like the idea of social insurance that's what socialism really is. The other is that any form of social insurance leads to socialism.

Social insurance – such as Social Security and Medicare – provides benefits paid for by the recipients themselves. Social insurance is a good thing. Hayek unequivocally commended social insurance in *The Road to Serfdom*.

Nor is there any reason why the state should not assist the individuals in providing for those common hazards of life against which, because of their uncertainty, few individuals can make adequate provision. Where, as in the case of sickness and accident, neither the desire to avoid such calamities nor efforts to overcome their consequences are as a rule weakened by the provision of assistance—where, in short, we deal with genuinely insurable risks—the case the for the state's helping to organize a comprehensive system of social insurance is very strong. … [T]here is no incompatibility in principle between the state's providing greater security in this way and the preservation of individual freedom.

The social (or Christian) democracies in Nordic Europe have freely chosen to offer a lot of social insurance. They are consistently the happiest countries in the world. That does not diminish their status as Capitalist nations.

Do not confuse "democratic Socialism" with "social democracy." Despite the superficial similarity they are two utterly different things. Nordic Europe is straight up Capitalist, with a vibrant business sector. There, true Capitalism is conjoined with a strong program of social insurance.

That's legitimate.

As an aside, the respect we, like Hayek, have for social democracy does not validate grotesque caricatures represented by such proposals as "Medicare for All." Medicare and Social Security are true social insurance. Beneficiaries pay modest annual premiums for many years. In return these premiums and their earnings are to provide for their old age.

In a climate of vibrant economic growth such as America enjoyed for decades after WWII and under Presidents Reagan and Clinton social insurance programs can be solvent forever.

They are not welfare. They are not entitlements. They are social insurance.

"Medicare for All," however, neglects to provide a viable, equitable, funding mechanism. Former Congressman and Democratic presidential candidate John Delaney called it "political suicide." He points out that if hospitals had to accept Medicare-level reimbursements, "some hospitals, especially struggling rural centers, would close virtually overnight, according to policy experts. Others, they say, would try to offset the steep cuts by laying off hundreds of thousands of workers and abandoning lower-paying services like mental health."

Even the reliably pro-social democracy editorial board of the *Washington Post* observed, along with other trenchant criticism,

> An <u>analysis of an earlier version</u> of [Sen. Bernie] Sanders's Medicare-for-all plan from the Urban Institute, a nonpartisan think tank, concluded that provider payment rates would have to be substantially higher, significantly raising the national health-care spending tab. Even then, care shortages would result. For his part, Mr. Blahous estimates an additional $5.4 trillion in spending if rates are more realistic. That would erase the $2 trillion in savings he projected under the rosiest scenario.

The proposed "Medicare for All" plans currently fashionable in the Democratic Party are neither democratic socialism nor social democracy. They are cyanide-laced policy Kool-Aid.

Socialism – the ownership of the means of production by the government – has failed wherever tried. Its remaining advocates attempt to avoid admitting this by claiming that nobody has actually tried real

Socialism. And that we should stick our hand into the buzz saw of Socialism yet again.

Lenin called these sorts "useful idiots."

The true name for the mixture of Big Business with the State is Fascism. Its emblem is an axe made of bundled sticks. Enemies of free markets like to slyly tar that as "right-wing."

There is nothing right about Fascism. Nor is there anything "right" about its even more evil twin, Nazism. Nazism was an abbreviation for National Socialism. Both were illiberal.

True Capitalism is liberal.

True Capitalists are committed to equitable prosperity. Their objective, in the words of Adam Smith, is universal opulence. It takes a genuine free market to create that. If prosperity is absent or inequitably distributed, true Capitalism is not there.

Even Marx and Engels, in *The Communist Manifesto*, pay homage to Capitalism's ability to conjure abundance:

> The bourgeoisie, during its rule of scarce one hundred years, has created more massive and more colossal productive forces than have all preceding generations together. Subjection of Nature's forces to man, machinery, application of chemistry to industry and agriculture, steam-navigation, railways, electric telegraphs, clearing of whole continents for cultivation, canalisation of rivers, whole populations conjured out of the ground – what earlier century had even a presentiment that such productive forces slumbered in the lap of social labour?

PART 2

CAPITALISM, THE ONLY ROAD TO UNIVERSAL OPULENCE

Earlier we defined capitalism and introduced its enemies, Socialists and even some of Capitalism's merchants. Let's refine the understanding.

Capital very much includes "human capital." That means people utilizing creativity, skills, and good health that enables them to produce. It is for this reason that universal health insurance, designed properly along market-based rather than centrally- planned principles, adds rather than subtracts from the wealth of the nation and to every member of society.

Marx and Engels, in inventing Communism, pitted the workers – the proletariat – against the middle class – the bourgeoisie. They claimed that the middle class was exploiting the workers.

Capitalism recognizes no classes or class struggle. Or to put it another way, true Capitalism is dedicated to universal opulence down to the lowest orders of society. That implies only one class: a great middle class.

In Capitalism, everyone can aspire to affluence through talent, hard work, and – yes – luck. Everyone owns their own capital. Everyone has the right – the dignity – of profiting from what they possess and from their own production. There will be differences in the level of affluence achieved. This will be due to differing levels of value we succeed in creating for others. And, yes, in part, due to luck.

If you create something that greatly improves the lives of a billion people it is just silly to begrudge you a few dollars, or even a few hundred dollars, from each of the beneficiaries.

Yes, some differences will be due to plain old dumb luck. Unless the game is rigged, that's not wrong. As President Kennedy once said,

> ...there is always inequity in life. Some men are killed in a war and some men are wounded, and some men never leave the country, and some men are stationed in the Antarctic and some are stationed in San Francisco. It's very hard in the military or personal life to assure complete equality. Life is unfair.
>
> –President's News Conference of March 21, 1962 (107), *Public Papers of the Presidents: John F. Kennedy, 1962.*

Good luck is not invidious. Since luck is blind it does not sustain righteous indignation.

That said, equal opportunity is a fundamental requirement of true Capitalism. Nobody is privileged or prejudiced based on social status or connections.

Status-based privilege and prejudice is Feudalism no matter what euphemism may mask it.

UNIVERSAL OPULENCE

True Capitalism generates a higher level of median affluence. Here's one vivid example.

Vice President Richard Nixon escorted Soviet Leader Nikita Khrushchev to the American National Exhibition in Moscow in 1959. They ended up in a high profile "kitchen debate" in a model kitchen. The debate was about the relative merits of Capitalism and Communism. As later recalled by then-publicist William Safire:

> I hollered at Major Hughes, 'This way to the typical American house!' ...
>
> Nixon: 'I want to show you this kitchen. It's like those of houses in California. See that built-in washing machine?'
>
> Khrushchev: 'We have such things.'
>
> Nixon: 'What we want to do is make more easy the life of our housewives.'
>
> Khrushchev: 'We do not have the capitalist attitude toward women.'
>
> ...
>
> Because the Russian press had derided the American claim that the house was affordable to workers — calling it 'a Taj Mahal' — Nixon noted that this house cost $14,000, and a government-guaranteed veterans mortgage made it possible for a steelworker earning $3 an hour to buy it for $100 a month. Khrushchev was

sarcastic: 'We have peasants who also can afford to spend $14,000 for a house.'"

Khrushchev's claims – "We have such things." And "We have peasants who also can afford to spend $14,000 for a house" – rang hollow. The standard of living of the USSR was far inferior to that of most of the workers in the USA. When Communism fell the living standards in the Russian Federation and former constituent republics began improving dramatically.

We contend that "you shall know a tree by its fruits." American factory workers then, under true Capitalism, could afford to own a fine modern home in a middle-class suburb for less than a quarter of their income. That shows the effect of true Capitalism.

The present struggle of American working families to subsist is evidence of the absence of true Capitalism. We detect the presence of Feudalism with a Capitalist façade.

The American worker's affluence of 1959 was not merely anecdotal. As *The Spectator* observed in an article titled <u>*Glad Tidings*</u> published in 2012:

> It may not feel like it, but 2012 has been the greatest year in the history of the world. That sounds like an extravagant claim, but it is borne out by evidence. Never has there been less hunger, less disease or more prosperity. The West remains in the economic doldrums, but most developing countries are charging ahead, and people are being lifted out of poverty at the fastest rate ever recorded. The death toll inflicted by war and natural disasters is also mercifully low. We are living in a golden age.

In 1990, the UN <u>announced</u> Millennium Development Goals, the first of which was to halve the number of people in extreme poverty by 2015. It <u>emerged this year</u> that the target was met in 2008. *Yet the achievement did not merit an official announcement, presumably because it was not achieved by any government scheme but by the pace of global Capitalism.* (Emphasis added.)

To drive this point even further home, note this from *The Conservative Review*:

> On November 13, 1979, the day Ronald Reagan <u>declared</u> <u>for the presidency</u>, the <u>Dow Jones Industrial Average was</u> <u>at 814</u>. (No, there's no comma missing.) It's now at 17,000. Supply-side having been picked up from America by many world leaders propelled world annual GDP, then around $11 trillion dollars in 1980, to over $60 trillion today. Trillion with a t.
>
> This does not adjust for inflation or population growth, both significant, yet still this gives some idea of the scope of prosperity ignited by supply-side economics. Not for no reason did I once <u>call its mastermind</u>, Prof. Robert Mundell, who later won the Nobel Prize in Economics, "The $100 Trillion Man."

And to gild the lily, in the seven years since this was written the Dow added nearly another 10,000 points. World GDP surged from $60T to $83T.

This is no anomaly. Recently, David Harsanyi, a Senior Editor at *The Federalist*, observed that nearly every quantifiable measure of human existence is improving. The retreat of socialism — exactly the kind of system environmentalists would like to bring back to fight global warming — has led to extraordinary gains in the most important aspects of human existence over the past 30-40 years.

Here are just a few:

Capitalism is eradicating extreme poverty.

...

It's eliminating child mortality.

...

It's increasing life expectancy.

...

It's mitigated conflicts — both internal and external.

...

It's keeping us safer...

...

...Even from guns.

...

It has made education more accessible.

…

And it's made us wealthier.

How?

Welcome to Capitalism at work.

HUMAN CAPITAL

From the same *Conservative Review* article quoted above:

> It would be powerful to put to work the work of the late Gary Becker, awarded the Nobel Memorial Prize in Economic Sciences in 1992 for his study of human capital. (The late Ted Schultz, also a Nobel Prize winner, also did important work in this area.)
>
> Becker was a professor of economics and sociology at the University of Chicago and the Booth School of Business.
>
> Wikipedia: "The best-known application of the idea of "human capital" in economics is that of Mincer and Gary Becker of the "Chicago School" of economics. Becker's book entitled Human Capital, published in 1964, became a standard reference for many years. In this view, human capital is similar to "physical means of production", e.g., factories and machines: one can invest in human capital (via education, training, medical treatment) and one's outputs depend partly on the rate of return on the human capital one owns."

21

Becker presented an entirely orthodox, yet extraordinarily innovative, approach to free market economic policy. Orthodox? Adam Smith defined human capital, in Book 2, Chapter 1, of *Wealth of Nations*:

> "Fourthly, of the acquired and useful abilities of all the inhabitants or members of the society. The acquisition of such talents, by the maintenance of the acquirer during his education, study, or apprenticeship, always costs a real expense, which is a capital fixed and realized, as it were, in his person. Those talents, as they make a part of his fortune, so do they likewise that of the society to which he belongs. The improved dexterity of a workman may be considered in the same light as a machine or instrument of trade which facilitates and abridges labor, and which, though it costs a certain expense, repays that expense with a profit."

...

> Human Capitalism is a policy treasure trove that has not yet been widely explored by political elites. And Human Capitalism is not "egghead" stuff.

I described it briefly in one of my recent *Forbes.com* columns:

Becker's work, call it Human Capitalism, would enlarge a supply side canon which, while valid, has grown somewhat stale. <u>Becker</u>:

To most people, capital means a bank account, a hundred shares of IBM stock, assembly lines, or steel plants in the Chicago area. These are all forms of capital in the sense that they are assets that yield income and other useful outputs over long periods of time.

But such tangible forms of capital are not the only type of capital. Schooling, a computer training course, expenditures on medical care, and lectures on the virtues of punctuality and honesty are also capital. That is because they raise earnings, improve health, or add to a person's good habits over much of his lifetime.

...

Education, training, and health are the most important investments in human capital.

(Let us add to this that having and raising children, arguably the gold standard of human capital, fits right into the Human Capitalism model.)

It would seem that the reflections made on Human Capitalism have merit.

A previous publication on the topic at Forbes.com by this author drew a tart riposte from Daniel Sankey in *People's World*, a socialist publication with a distinguished pedigree as the direct descendant of the Daily Worker, then reprinted by the <u>Communist Party of Northern California</u>:

An article recently written in Forbes by a Mr. Ralph Benko proposes 'human capitalism' as the solution to the shrinking wages and economic stagnation in the U.S.

Human Capitalism, briefly described, is to treat investments in workers with the same seriousness and enthusiasm that investments in factories and machinery receive.

Simply put, the author argues that investments in the training and education of U.S. workers is essential.

He then goes on to praise Bernie Sanders' sincerity in fighting for the working class while at the same time deploring the senator's socialist solutions.

Socialism he argues, echoing the ignorant self-satisfaction of most neoliberal capitalists, simply doesn't work.

Like all good capitalists, Mr. Benko believes we can have our cake and eat it too.

We can have record profits for the one percent while at the same time producing good jobs for everyone else. …

While I applaud anyone who believes in the importance of investing in workers, I question his sincerity and his understanding of socialist economics.

No grounds for questioning our sincerity. As true Capitalists our commitment to universal opulence is ferocious. And there is no good reason to question our understanding of the blood-dimmed tide of Socialist economics.

Feudalism by any other name would smell as rank.

In aptly dubbing Bill and Melinda Gates the world's greatest leaders *Fortune* salutes their commitment to human capital:

> **It was March 2018, and once more Bill Gates** found himself behind a podium. In the previous few months, he had given one keynote address after another—in San Francisco, he'd urged drugmakers to focus on diseases that affect the poor as well as the rich; in Andhra Pradesh, India, he had preached the value of smallholder farms; in Abu Dhabi, he'd enjoined the Crown Prince and other princelings to continue their financial support for global health initiatives; in Cleveland, he'd promoted investment in better schools.
>
> Now the world's second-richest man and foremost itinerant advocate for the poor was in Abuja, Nigeria, talking about the same theme that had underlain all of these speeches: the need to invest in "human capital."

The future of capitalism is human capitalism.

THE SECRET INGREDIENTS OF PROSPERITY

Every Capitalist enterprise, without fail, comprises four categories. There is *capital*, the means of production. There is *labor*, those who work to build the products or provide the services. There are the *materials* employed by capital and labor to create finished products. There are the *means to market*, sell, and deliver the products.

That's it.

It's the way the world works. Nothing more. Nothing less. Pretending otherwise is either obfuscation or confusion.

Marx and Engels in their little *Manifesto* posited the notion that Capitalism destroyed Feudalism. Right on! They declared that Communism would in turn destroy Capitalism. Not so much.

The dictatorship of the proletariat was, they declared, certain to destroy the oppressor bourgeoisie. That would produce a lovely Communist economy. They promised that this would result in a Socialist workers' paradise. And that the State would wither away, an unnecessary artifact.

Didn't work out in practice. Rather the opposite.

PEOPLE VS. THE MONSTROUS STATE

Under Socialism, especially Communism, the State grew to monstrous, all-pervading proportions. Workers found themselves mired in a Socialist workers' Hell. Marx and Engels stated that the aim was to take the next evolutionary leap. They looked to get past 19th-century industrial Capitalism.

Their archaic 19th-century vision remains to this day the true heartbeat of the left. It's painful to watch. How many times must Lucy yank away the football before Charlie Brown quits her sadistic game?

Socialism turned out in practice to be lipstick on the pig of Feudalism. It was and is a throwback in which the powerful and affluent have – and keep – all the power and affluence. In Feudalism the nobles, in Socialism the apparatchiks of the Communist Party, had all the power and most of the goodies.

Socialism denies workers' agency and even dignity. Socialism forces the majority of workers into long lines for scarce necessities: bare subsistence.

Whereas under Capitalism the shops are full. Whereas Capitalism provides true agency to all.

Socialism is not progress. Progress means the betterment of the general welfare. That demonstrably comes only from Capitalism.

Ludwig von Mises, in his big book *Human Action*, describes at length the essence of true Capitalism. To oversimplify, Mises argues that "all action is a response to a felt lack." Those who can profitably supply that lack will prosper.

Human Action is almost a thousand pages long. Harry Gordon Selfridge, a great merchant and great and true Capitalist, summed up the essence of Capitalism in just five words:

The customer is always right.

To summarize, in true Capitalism the customer is king.

And YOU are the customer. What you want matters. If you want "green" solutions and coffee not produced by virtual slave labor, for instance, YOU ARE KING. Informed consumer demand is far more powerful than any regulation, which is why a free press and free speech are vital to Capitalism.

Supply and demand, and nothing else, determine the price of everything. No subgroup of buyers or sellers can control the price of things for very long.

The legend of King Canute portrayed him as humbly demonstrating his lack of power by commanding the incoming tide to halt. It was an act of humility in which he was intentionally demonstrating his powerlessness. It was an act of humility that most of our political leaders have yet to grasp.

Markets are as powerful as the tides. They may be harnessed. Never commanded.

Marx and Engels promised a withering away of the state. Perversely, their path to eliminating the state was to create a monstrous, overbearing, and monolithic state. Their scheme never worked. Whoever would have guessed that tyranny is not the path to liberty?

THE INVISIBLE HAND

This leads us to the "invisible hand," a trope that Adam Smith made famous. It is a mystical hand that creates the complex relationships needed to meet all society's needs. It adapts, grows, invents, and changes to meet those changing needs under changing circumstances.

Smith:

> [The rich] consume little more than the poor, and in spite of their natural selfishness and rapacity...they divide with the poor the produce of all their improvements. They are led by an invisible hand to make nearly the same distribution of the necessaries of life, which would have been made, had the earth been divided into equal portions among all its inhabitants, and thus without intending it, without knowing it, advance the interest of the society, and afford means to the multiplication of the species.

The free market – true Capitalism – is the most efficient way to distribute and sell products. It is the most efficient way to develop new products which meet new needs or which better satisfy old needs. Or as Say's Law has it, "Supply creates its own demand."

It is the best way to ensure freedom for the individual to buy and sell as he or she pleases. This is not a counsel of callousness toward the have-nots. It does not imply tolerance of profiteers or polluters.

It does imply a certain wry skepticism as to the premise of Socialism: the ability of government officials to generate equitable prosperity.

Smith, again:

> It is the highest impertinence and presumption… in kings and ministers, to pretend to watch over the economy of private people, and to restrain their expense… They are themselves always, and without any exception, the greatest spendthrifts in the society. Let them look well after their own expense, and they may safely trust private people with theirs. If their own extravagance does not ruin the state, that of their subjects never will.

The perfect democracy is the free market. Regulated only to prevent fraud or other fouls (like pollution), a free market is the least subject to rigging by those already privileged.

CAPITALISM IS A POSITIVE-SUM GAME

Is it possible for the wealthy to make even more money while workers also make more money? Yes. Wealth is not a static thing for people to fight over. Only under Feudalism does more for you mean less for me.

Wealth, under true Capitalism, is organic. Nurtured, wealth will grow for everyone. Universal opulence is the achievable goal. Under true Capitalism there is no limit to the possibilities for wealth creation. Yes, some things have limited supplies. That said, inventors have consistently been able to find ways to do more with less.

Today, for a few hundred dollars almost everyone has a device in their pocket that has more computing power than the entire Apollo moon program. The computing power of a mobile phone <u>would</u> <u>have cost</u> around $32 million in the mid-1980s (and, before that taken up whole rooms).

Thanks to true Capitalism, we take this sort of thing for granted. Steve Jobs – who immediately grasped the uses of 5 gigabytes in a tiny space – didn't sell the original iPod as a gizmo. He sold it as "a thousand songs in your pocket." And delivered.

If we adopt truer and truer Capitalism we will dramatically increase equitable prosperity over the next generation. We will increase the general welfare exponentially. And the injured prestige of Capitalism will recover.

Wealth is as abundant as the wind or sunlight. When we act as if wealth is a static thing to be doled out frugally we retard the creation of new wealth. The mindset that there can only be a few wealthy people prevents people from achieving full potential.

Socialism has a beggar's mentality. It asks from us for as much as possible while offering each of us as little as possible. And the zero-sum game of "we will continue to pretend to work as long as you continue to pretend to pay us" of Socialism makes workers poorer.

It is liberating to put away this delusion of wealth as a static thing.

Let's take full advantage of the tremendous leveraging power of participatory economics. Participatory is exactly what Capitalism is. Capitalism offers, as Adam Smith said and which bears repeating, "universal opulence which extends itself to the lowest ranks of the people."

This is not a counsel of passivity or callousness. This does not suggest that we should be indifferent to poverty or inequity. To the contrary.

POVERTY AND INEQUITY ARE WRONG

Poverty and inequity are wrong.

Their persistence calls for a forceful remedy.

That remedy is true Capitalism. Human action.

Not Socialism.

Not government action.

Many members of the privileged elite masquerade under the mask of "free markets" while subverting true Capitalism. In writing the mission statement for the *National Review* William F. Buckley had a tart word for those he dismissed as "the well-fed Right":

> Radical conservatives in this country have an interesting time of it, for when they are not being suppressed or mutilated by the Liberals, they are being ignored or humiliated by a great many of those of the well-fed Right, whose ignorance and amorality have never been exaggerated for the same reason that one cannot exaggerate infinity.

So-called Capitalism without a free market is a fraud. Without free markets there can be no free enterprise. There can be no universal opulence. There can be no freedom itself.

We require Capitalism and free markets – together, true Capitalism – to enjoy the "liberty and justice for all" to which we are all pledged. Enter the spirit of Capitalism Future.

Once upon a time, Capitalism conveyed, in common parlance, the industrialism of steel mills and automobile assembly lines. Technology is changing that.

Human Capitalism is emerging. People's health, education, and welfare are becoming recognized as capital equal to or of greater value than that of factories. Let us treat these assets as such.

Thus, capital and labor begin to converge. Socialism is not the next step up from Capitalism. Socialism is a step backward. Socialism has proved itself to be, in practice, Feudalism. Feudalism drenches the privileged with more privilege. For the rest of us it offers only subsistence.

Human creativity, innovation and initiative are the most important factors in creating wealth. Here's one striking example from that great anticipatory design scientist R. Buckminster Fuller who wrote, in *Critical Path*, in 1981:

> Humanity's cosmic-energy income account consists entirely of our gravity-and star (99 percent Sun)-distributed cosmic dividends of water power, tidal power, wave power, wind power, vegetation-produced alcohols, methane gas, vulcanism, and so on. Humanity's present rate of total energy consumption amounts to only one

four-millionth of one percent of the rate of its energy income.

Tax-hungry government and profit-hungry business, for the moment, find it insurmountably difficult to arrange to put meters between humanity and its cosmic energy income, and thus they do nothing realistic to help humanity enjoy its fabulous energy-income wealth.

Imagine that! We only use four-millionth of one percent of the energy available to us. This is a counsel of abundance.

The newly-minted Simon Abundance Index demonstrates this consistently. A clear commitment to creativity by preserving, protecting, and defending true Capitalism is the path to universal affluence.

It is the only such path. Not Socialism.

PART 3

THE NEW FEUDALISM; SOCIALISM AND CRONYISM

WHAT IS FEUDALISM?

Feudalism rewards people based on their social status. True Capitalism rewards people based on their contribution to the general welfare. Now, the Feudalists are attempting to pin their sins, especially inequitable outcomes, on Capitalism. This is a big lie.

Under Feudalism, royals, nobles and aristocrats lived high on the hog. Peasants ate bread by the sweat of their brow. The privileges of the elites were not gained or lost on the merits. The prejudices against working people were not due to earned demerits.

Opulence was largely derived from social status under Feudalism. Capitalism, with its propensity to create universal opulence, instead rewards merit and achievement. Today, what is called Capitalism is degenerating into a status-based system. Let's call the encroaching system the ghost of Capitalism present neo- Feudalism.

Under Feudalism there were "sumptuary laws" that forbade lower classes from even purchasing or displaying products of opulence, such as certain types of clothes or means of conveyance, or houses! Thus even if one garnered wealth through hard work their enjoyment of opulence was limited by law.

The history of human civilization is the tale of the conquest of Feudalism by Capitalism. Capitalism frees people through creativity and innovation. Feudalists (sometimes called tyrants, dictators, or despots) keep people under their control through fear. They also use fraud: empty promises.

Tyrants recognize Capitalism as a threat to their arbitrary power. So, they defame it.

From the dawn of civilization Capitalists by whatever name sought to serve the greatest number in the greatest possible ways. They sought a reasonable profit in return. Totalitarians sought and seek to exploit as many as possible to the maximum extent possible for their own unbridled power and profit.

The correct judge of what is equitable is not a sword-bearer who forces you to buy at the king's price. The only correct judge is the customer who must be free to buy or not.

Libels and slanders have turned the word Capitalism into a confusing buzzword. The abuse of the word Capitalism by exploiters who seek to hide their tricks under a noble brand have compounded the felony.

Adam Smith did not use the word Capitalism. Yet he wrote the original definitive guide to free enterprise. Smith described a moral system, one best promoting the general welfare. He never advocated the privileging of the owners of the means of production nor the exploitation of the workers. Rather the contrary.

Karl Marx popularized the term Capitalism. He meant it as a pejorative. To oversimplify, he attacked it as a system that oppressed workers. He propounded Communism as a way to give a fairer deal to workers. And he prescribed ruthless means for the workers — the proletariat — to emancipate themselves from Capitalist "oppression."

The Communist revolutionaries and tyrants were exemplified by Stalin and Pol Pot. They killed tens of millions, by some reckonings 100 million. They did this, they claimed, to bring about the Socialist Workers' Paradise.

Rather than building a classless society they generated a new class, "the nomenklatura." These were the operatives of the Communist Party. The promised paradise — economic security and a decent affluence — always failed to materialize for the workers.

The Communist leadership blamed the Capitalists for that. They still do. But a sports franchise that loses every game would at some point fire its manager and scrap its playbook. Blaming the other team only goes so far.

The romantic appeal of Communism to the elites (who were and would be the governors of such a system) never goes away. As we write this yet another *Communist Manifesto* is in press, garnering favorable attention from prestige publications such as *The New York Times*. It is entitled *Fully Automated Luxury Communism: A Manifesto*. An excerpt:

> Automation, robotics and machine learning will, as many august bodies, from the Bank of England to the White House, have predicted, substantially shrink the

work force, creating widespread technological unemployment. But that's only a problem if you think work — as a cashier, driver or construction worker — is something to be cherished. For many, work is drudgery. And automation could set us free from it.

Gene editing and sequencing could revolutionize medical practice, moving it from reactive to predictive. Hereditary diseases could be eliminated, including Huntington's disease, cystic fibrosis and sickle cell anemia, and cancer cured before it reaches Stage 1. Those technologies could allow us to keep pace with the health challenges presented by societal aging — by 2020 there will be more people over the age of 60 than under the age of 5 — and even to surpass them.

What's more, renewable energy, which has been experiencing steep annual falls in cost for half a century, could meet global energy needs and make possible the vital shift away from fossil fuels. More speculatively, asteroid mining — whose technical barriers are presently being surmounted — could provide us with not only more energy than we can ever imagine but also more iron, gold, platinum and nickel. Resource scarcity would be a thing of the past.

The consequences are far-reaching and potentially transformative. For the crises that confront our world today — technological unemployment, global poverty, societal aging, climate change, resource scarcity — we can already glimpse the remedy.

But there's a catch. It's called Capitalism. It has created the newly emerging abundance, but it is unable to share round the fruits of technological development.

There they go again. The new Communists, just like Marx and Engels, acknowledge Capitalism's power to create abundance. Then they slyly indict Capitalism for its inability to "share round the fruits."

This overlooks the fact that all but the poorest of the poor in developed – Capitalist – countries tend to own cell phones, color TVs, and live in air-conditioned and centrally-heated homes with plentiful food.

As Tim Worstall writing in *Forbes.com* – that Capitalist Tool! – noted a few years back, "the average American today is 90 Times Richer than the Average Historical Human Being."

> I have regularly tried to get over the idea that there is just no such thing as real poverty in the United States today. Absent those entirely outside our society through addiction or mental health problems there is just no one at all who suffers from what has been the usual human description of poverty. Actually, there's no one at all in the US who has anything even close to what the human experience has been of poverty. By any historical, and by standards of all too large a part of the world today, all Americans are simply hugely, gargantuanly, richer than any but the fewest, most privileged, of our forefathers.

Capitalism, and with it the "universal opulence which extends itself to the lowest ranks of the people," strikes again!

"Unable to share round the fruits?" Simply untrue to the point of inanity. How inconvenient a truth for those who wish to restore the neo-Feudalism that is Communism or Socialism. So they ignore it.

Back to the *New Oxford American Dictionary*. Communism is defined as "a society in which all property is publicly owned and each person works and is paid according to their abilities and needs."

Who runs the government, the steward of "publicly owned" property? People. There is no evidence that the civil servants who staff the government are more virtuous or talented than those who work in the private sector. Societies in which "all property is publicly owned" have not worked to improve the public welfare.

Socialism, like Communism, is just lingering romantic utopianism, a theory discredited in practice. Equitable prosperity, albeit imperfect, is a hallmark of Capitalism, not Communism nor Socialism.

As Sir Winston Churchill summed it up neatly in a <u>speech in the House of Commons</u> on October 22, 1945, "The inherent vice of Capitalism is the unequal sharing of blessings. The inherent virtue of Socialism is the equal sharing of miseries."

For much of human history the true Capitalist has faced totalitarian opposition and interference. This has caused great human misery. Religion, racism, tribalism, and fanaticism have proven less the cause of war and destruction than Feudalism, very much including Communism. The Communists, beginning with Marx and Engels, prescribed despotism to liberate the workers from oppression by the middle class. This unleashed horrors.

CAPITALISM IS THE DIAMETRIC OPPOSITE OF CRONYISM

Socialism and its more virulent form, Communism, is not Capitalism's sole enemy. It bears repeating Adam Smith and Friedrich Hayek warned us that some wealthy capitalists are another such enemy. Among the latter we find cronyism. Cronyism means handing out rewards based on family or social connections.

Such rewards are inequitably distributed. The rewards include the best jobs, prestige media exposure, the best investment opportunities, and admission to elite colleges and clubs. These are a few examples. Another example of cronyism would be "corporate welfare."

That's the manipulation of the political leadership by rich and powerful corporations to gain subsidies and special privileges. It's a bad thing.

Cronyism is by definition strictly anti-capitalist. Capitalism is by its very nature opposed to cronyism in all forms. Some people have tried to re-label cronyism as "crony capitalism." That's a sly slur. It is usually made by Socialists or Progressives to tarnish the reputation of Capitalism.

Let's take a closer look. Obviously "crony capitalism" is an oxymoron. Oxymorons are a coupling of antonyms, like "hot cold" or "living dead." Cronyism and Capitalism cannot coexist. True Capitalism has equality of opportunity baked right in. True Capitalism has no tolerance for status-based or relationship-based privilege.

Cronyism in the business and political world exists. It has nothing to do with true Capitalism. It is a corruption of Capitalism.

What do Cronyism, Socialism, Fascism, Communism and even National Socialism have in common? They are all variants of Feudalism.

In all forms of Feudalism, a ruling class has political and social mastery over lower classes. Power and prestige, not meritorious service to the general welfare, are the foundation of such mastery.

Feudalist leaders correctly perceive true Capitalism as a mortal threat. All Feudalisms, by whatever name, relentlessly suppress, subvert, or corrupt true Capitalism. It is a threat to the hegemony of their elites.

Cronyism is not an ideology. It is a manifestation of greed. The political and commercial elite seek to control the lives of the workers, voters and consumers from sheer selfishness.

Cronyism is rarely candid about its corrupt nature. It pretends – even to itself -- to be rooted in merit. The evidence proves otherwise.

As Chris Ryan writes in his book *Civilized to Death*, recently excerpted at *Wired Magazine* in an article headlined <u>*Why Are Rich People So Mean?*</u>:

> In one of my favorite studies, Keltner and Piff decided to tweak a game of Monopoly. The psychologists rigged the game so that one player had huge advantages over the other from the start. They ran the study with over a hundred pairs of subjects, all of whom were brought into the lab where a coin was flipped to determine who'd be "rich" and "poor" in the game. The randomly chosen "rich" player started out with twice as much money, collected twice as much every time they went around the board, and got to roll two dice instead of one. None of these advantages was hidden from the players. Both were well aware of how unfair the situation was. But still, the "winning" players showed the tell-tale symptoms of Rich Asshole Syndrome. They were far more

likely to display dominant behaviors like smacking the board with their piece, loudly celebrating their superior skill, even eating more pretzels from a bowl positioned nearby.

After 15 minutes, the experimenters asked the subjects to discuss their experience of playing the game. When the rich players talked about why they'd won, they focused on their brilliant strategies rather than the fact that the whole game was rigged to make it nearly impossible for them to lose. "What we've been finding across dozens of studies and thousands of participants across this country," said Piff, "is that as a person's levels of wealth increase, their feelings of compassion and empathy go down, and their feelings of entitlement, of deservingness, and their ideology of self-interest increases."

Ayn "Virtue of Selfishness" Rand call your office!

Socialists opportunistically exploit the opportunistic infection by cronyism to defame Capitalism. This is like using HIV to impugn helper T-cells.

Socialists conduct a classic "bait and switch" maneuver. The "reformers" then make themselves the new ruling elite. As the new rulers they then harvest the fruits of cronyism for themselves

… and their cronies!

They make the matter of the workers' struggle for economic security even worse. How? As even orthodox Communists admit Socialism is inferior for the production of wealth. The transition to that neo-Feudalism called Socialism leaves less to distribute. That further weakens society's ability to realize the Capitalist goal of universal opulence to the lowest ranks.

After "the revolution," Socialism and Communism inevitably worsen the social morbidities and injustices exploited to accuse the previous regime of illegitimacy. But as the late Henry Wallach once wryly observed, "Experience is the name we give to our past mistakes, reform that we give to future ones."

There is no excuse for cronyism. All true Capitalists despise it. And we are more militant than Socialists in opposing it. Why? Out of self-respect. Socialists weaponize cronyism to tarnish the Capitalist brand.

So the next time you hear someone attacking "crony capitalism" set them straight. Cronyism and Capitalism are antithetical.

Cronyism and Socialism are redundant. Socialism is just Cronyism on steroids.

Cronyism is a corruption of Capitalism. It often uses Capitalist rhetoric while subverting Capitalist principles. And yet, even with cronyist subversion some market forces remain active. Cronyism diminishes (and delegitimizes) free enterprise. Yet some level of opportunity remains.

Moreover, as François de La Rochefoucauld observed, "hypocrisy is the tribute that vice pays to virtue." Cronyists under Capitalism pay at least a hypocritical tribute to Capitalism. That provides a foothold for true Capitalists to fight back.

Greed is not good. Greed is not the foundation of Capitalism. Capitalism abjures greed. All claims to the contrary are but a sly slur by the enemies of equal opportunity and universal opulence that is true Capitalism. Integrity, honor, service, respect for the human dignity of all people as well as equal opportunity and a commitment to universal opulence are as central to capitalism as are the laws of supply and demand.

True Capitalism rewards people in proportion to their service to others. It is the opposite of greed. And in fact the rewards to the Capitalist are exponentially smaller than the rewards the Capitalist visits upon society.

In Socialist circles it long has been the fashion to conflate cronyism with capitalism. Socialist propagandists then proceed to deconstruct cronyism as a straw man for Capitalism.

Socialists misrepresent Capitalism as an altar to Moloch. They present Capitalism as an evil idol. They misrepresent it as a malevolent force. They lie that there we sacrifice the financial and social welfare of the people and the environment.

Allen Ginsberg, in *Howl*:

> *Moloch the incomprehensible prison! Moloch the crossbone soulless jailhouse and Congress of sorrows!*

This is a libel.

How identical in tone and sentiment to the Communist indictment of capitalism which continues unabated as attested at leftvoice.org:

> Climate change and the crises of the biological cycles of carbon, water, phosphorus and nitrogen; the acidification of the oceans; the accelerated loss of biodiversity; the changes in the quality of soil and chemical pollution by industry—these are some of the terrible expressions of a completely unprecedented situation for humanity, namely the tendency toward the destruction of our natural conditions for production and reproduction.

Communists are still whitewashing the moldering remains of the ecocide they wrought at the height of their power.

Few Socialists could withstand a close examination of their character of life any better than any businessmen. Socialism chronically fails to deliver anything but subsistence and often misery. Socialism has proved itself – not Capitalism -- to be "the incomprehensible prison."

Capitalism supports benevolence for the needy. Capitalism welcomes public spending for the general welfare and humanitarian causes. Post-communist Chinese Chairman Deng Xiaoping once observed, "Poverty is not socialism."

We say that generosity is not socialism. Yes, Socialists purport to be generous with other people's money (until it runs out). Rarely, if ever, are Socialists generous with their own money. Socialist generosity is usually a ruse to get their hands on your money for their own aggrandizement.

Socialists, in pursuit of political power and social privilege, pretend to compassion. Cronyists, already privileged and ensconced within the system that privileged them, dispense with pretense. We don't know which is worse.

That said, we demand that political and economic systems be judged on their outcomes rather than their intentions. "The road to Hell is paved with good intentions."

The more truly Capitalist a society, the greater the general welfare. The greater the trend toward universal opulence.

Socialism destroys equitable prosperity. Cronyism degrades it.

Capitalism is not Cronyism.

Capitalism is the opposite of Cronyism.

FEUDALISTS ARE LEGION

Feudalists have more names and identities than one can imagine. From "left" or "right" they always offer fear in one hand and empty, usually fraudulent, promises of something for nothing in the other.

The Capitalist relies instead on a fair and free market to serve people at a justified profit. The Capitalist asks for nothing more than opportunity and recognizes that justice is best served by leaving it up to each of us to decide what is in our own best interests.

True Capitalism gives everyone equal and abundant means to acquire their necessities, amenities, and even luxuries. If I can afford luxuries by providing you with necessities that's a good thing, not a bad one. True Capitalism relies on the demands of free people — customers — to determine what to sell and how much to pay.

Yes, that can degenerate into "consumerism." Consumerism is a degenerate form of materialism. It's a Capitalist heresy. Materialism detaches Capitalism from morality and must be fought. Still, it is important to recognize Consumerism as a caricature of Capitalism, not true Capitalism.

A legion of tyrants, often tolerated and even supported by the very people held in bondage, resists true Capitalism. Socialists have often won elections. Unscrupulous merchants exploit naive or unwary buyers. Call it what you will. Socialists or anti-Capitalist merchants are still Feudalist.

Whatever the totalitarian "product," it always has three legs. It plays on fear. It offers things it cannot deliver and it privileges the few at the expense of the many, never giving fair value.

"Democratic Socialism" is a euphemism for soft totalitarianism. Socialism, like Communism, is a form of fraud with which to pillage the credulous.

WHO IS A CAPITALIST?

The true Capitalist uses creativity to innovate ways to improve people's lives. Profit is the sign that the provider is generating more value than she is consuming. Human creativity — and nothing else — sows the seeds of prosperity for all. The true Capitalist mindset is one of serving people, leaving people free to take or leave the offering. The more people within a society with this mindset the better off the community.

The Capitalist calls to people and says, "these are my wares, buy them if you wish." The Feudal baron sends says, "You must give me whatever I dictate based on whatever flimsy pretext I declare."

The history of humanitarian progress comes down to a history of the Capitalist impulse. It's the story of freedom versus the totalitarian urge for domination. The true Capitalist alone offers freedom. The Feudal baron may use the rhetoric of justice, equality, or noble motivation. But the Feudal baron cannot produce anything like what the Capitalist can produce. The baron exploits rather than enhances the lives of the people.

Yes, there are degrees of Feudalism. Some operate on a misappropriated Capitalist brand. Some call themselves Socialists. Either way, history has proven that there is no substitute for true Capitalism for producing a free, equitable, and prosperous society: universal opulence.

Capitalists and The Political Parties: What's the political agenda for free market Capitalism in the 21ˢᵗ century?

As I, William Collier, write I am visiting Friedrich Engels Straße in Ludwigsburg, Germany. It's an appropriate place to be writing a refutation of *The Communist Manifesto*. We aspire to a higher cause: pointing the way forward to an agenda that can bring about universal opulence.

One of his disciples asked Jesus, "Who will be the greatest?" Jesus answered that whoever served others would be the greatest. That's also the precise formula for unleashing equitable prosperity through true Capitalism. Those who serve the needs of others the most are the greatest of all and the most deserving of honor.

If the most talented, hardest working, and most virtuous people consistently aren't rising to the top economically and socially, however, it's a warning sign. If those with the best ideas, products, and services are not thriving, it's a portent. Inequity prevailing says that the free market has been disrupted, preventing the service of others honorably and organically.

All forms of Socialism are the opposite of freedom. The cultural appropriation of the language of democracy is an insult to workers and people of conscience everywhere.

Modern progressives promise democracy and equality through heavy taxation. They prescribe redistribution — by themselves, rather than by the markets — of the wealth created by the industrious. They propose to put government officials in charge of regulating commerce. They are busy installing controls on our very thinking. Orwell predicted these thought police concocting and punishing thoughtcrimes.

If all this sounds like the modern version of Feudalism, you're pretty darn woke. Or, if you prefer, perceptive. So what can we expect from that progressive Neo-Feudalism called democratic Socialism? As *The Who* sang: "Meet the new boss. Same as the old boss."

True Capitalism doesn't promise a "withering away of the state." It offers to downsize the government so that it can best perform its healthy, natural, and organic functions. These include "to form a more perfect union, establish justice, insure domestic tranquility, provide for the common defense, promote the general welfare, and secure the blessings of liberty to ourselves and our posterity."

The gargantuan "warfare/welfare" state which is a leftover of a century of world wars is, today, unjustified and unjustifiable. True Capitalists oppose all of its attendant privileges, all rewards based on social status rather than merit. We oppose the exploitation of the people by their self-anointed betters.

RESISTANCE TO FEUDALISM IS NOT FUTILE

To the Socialists among you we call you out as the Feudalists you are. We expect your spirited and determined resistance.

We expect you to fight dirty, with lies and misrepresentations of our motives and our track record. You always have misrepresented us. Why would you change that now?

Bring it on.

We aim to overthrow the Socialist political, social, and cultural hegemony. We plan to confront and defeat you in all of your strongholds of power and oppression. The road from serfdom is sure to be fraught with ferocious opposition. And yet the resurgence and victory of true Capitalism in its 21ˢᵗ century manifestation is close to inevitable.

As Thomas Paine, attacking the legitimacy of monarchy, the apotheosis of privilege, wrote in *The American Crisis*:

> **THESE** are the times that try men's souls.
>
> The summer soldier and the sunshine patriot will, in this crisis, shrink from the service of their country; but he that stands it now, deserves the love and thanks of man and woman.
>
> Tyranny, like hell, is not easily conquered; yet we have this consolation with us, that the harder the conflict, the more glorious the triumph.
>
> What we obtain too cheap, we esteem too lightly: it is dearness only that gives every thing its value.
>
> Heaven knows how to put a proper price upon its goods; and it would be strange indeed if so celestial an article as **freedom** should not be highly rated.

The spirit of freedom that replaced the domination of Feudalism with the trend toward the universal opulence of Capitalism lives in the hearts and minds of millions. It is the aspiration of billions. This spirit is the driving force that will bury your Neo-Feudalism which can only, at best, deliver to the masses a grinding subsistence.

The people eventually will realize that only true Capitalism delivers universal opulence. Only in a universally affluent and free society will class and prejudice wither away. Old grievances and wounds are being opened afresh by the left, committed, à la Marx, to class warfare.

Socialists are out to make people fearful, angry, and easily manipulated. Indeed, as the great H.L. Mencken wrote in *In Defense of Women*:

> Civilization, in fact, grows more and more maudlin and hysterical; especially under democracy it tends to degenerate into a mere combat of crazes; the whole aim of practical politics is to keep the populace alarmed (and hence clamorous to be led to safety) by menacing it with an endless series of hobgoblins, most of them imaginary."

Don't fall for it.

PART 4

THE RADICAL IMPERATIVE OF CAPITALISM

THE AIM OF TRUE CAPITALISM IS UNIVERSAL OPULENCE

The left likes to parade the imaginary hobgoblin that Capitalists value profits over people. Preposterous! The aim of true Capitalism is universal opulence. Universal as in *for everybody.*

Any other outcome than universal opulence, whether at the hand of a phony Capitalist (a crony feudalist, if you will) or that of a real Socialist, is a perversion. True Capitalists are dedicated to the general welfare because, in the end, the greatest among us is he or she who is of greatest service to the most people. This is Capitalism!

And what of nationalism vs. globalism?

Let's go back to our core root. The highest object of affection for the true Capitalist is happy people in a sustainable environment. Period. The issue is not one of nationalism versus globalism. It is, as always, one of free markets versus the various oppressions inherent in Feudalism and the Neo-Feudalism of the Socialists as well as the merchants pretending to be Capitalists, the cronies.

Free markets free us all. They do not countenance the exploitation of one group by another. Exploitation does not equal profit. Exploitation equals plunder.

The point is not whether one is a globalist or a nationalist. One is either a true, free market, Capitalist or one is a Feudalist of one or more shades and distinctions. There is only one form of Capitalism versus a dizzying array of forms of Feudalism.

The perfect and ideal goal is a global free market economy. The purpose of a global free market is global abundance. It is "liberty and justice for all," including the elimination of all forms of political oppression and social inequity.

Nor does Capitalism countenance pollution. Pollution is antithetical to happiness and destructive of opulence. Pollution of the environment is a violation of the general welfare. It should be treated as the crime that it is. True Capitalism is sustainable. It makes the Earth greener.

The left loves to posture for justice. Their activists fancy themselves "Social Justice Warriors." The right loves to focus on liberty. But the Pledge of Allegiance, which we all – left and right – have taken countless times concludes with a commitment to "liberty and justice for all."

Liberty and justice are complementary, not antagonistic, values.

THE HAPPINESS AGENDA

Meanwhile, true Capitalists, whether their political leanings be left or right, tend to focus energy on the pursuit of happiness. Pursuit of happiness is a quintessentially American value, declared in the Declaration of Independence.

True Capitalists don't care about your ancestry. Alexander Hamilton, a quintessential Capitalist, was born in the most modest of circumstances. Feudalists judge you by your social status. Capitalists judge you on your merits, including your moral courage.

We want people, all people, to be happy and to enjoy affluence. We want people, including ourselves, to flourish by playing a role in advancing the happiness agenda.

The truly free market is no threat to anybody's way of life. A truly free market is inherently just and equitable. Regardless of past privileges or prejudices, the free market is the secret recipe to unleash prosperity. President Kennedy called this "the rising tide" that "lifts all boats."

The Capitalist movement has ample room for social democrats as well as conservatives. The only litmus test is whether you are committed, for yourself and others, to the pursuit of happiness and human dignity rather than privilege and power.

WHETHER YOU ARE A CONSERVATIVE OR A LIBERAL

If you advance true Capitalism as the path to universal opulence and if your desired outcomes are purely related to working within and through the free market you have come to the right place. True Capitalism has ample room for both the left, which prioritizes equity, and the right, which prioritizes prosperity so long as both values are honored and the mechanism to achieve both – free markets – is honored.

Our critique of any policy or agenda will always come down to: does it advance true free market Capitalism and does it seek to achieve its aims through serving the needs of people honorably and ethically.

Does this seem simple? Good. Because it is!

This is a simple, powerful test. It will always dispel the smoke and mirrors of the doublespeak and doublethink of Feudalists everywhere.

Call it crowdsourcing. Call it a representative democracy. Call it classical liberal republicanism. Call it the rising tide. Let the people determine their own destiny in the free market of ideas, goods and services, and politics.

Under true Capitalism we are the masters of our fate.

THE SOCIALIST TEN COMMANDMENTS

Marx and Engels call for the abolition of the family and the abolition of religion. And *The Communist Manifesto* puts forth the "Ten Commandments" of Communism. They explicitly call for "despotic inroads" to bring about:

1. Abolition of property in land and application of all rents of land to public purposes.
2. A heavy progressive or graduated income tax.
3. Abolition of all rights of inheritance.
4. Confiscation of the property of all emigrants and rebels.
5. Centralisation of credit in the hands of the state, by means of a national bank with State capital and an exclusive monopoly.
6. Centralisation of the means of communication and transport in the hands of the State.

7. Extension of factories and instruments of production owned by the State; the bringing into cultivation of waste- lands, and the improvement of the soil generally in accordance with a common plan.
8. Equal liability of all to work. Establishment of industrial armies, especially for agriculture.
9. Combination of agriculture with manufacturing industries; gradual abolition of all the distinction between town and country by a more equable distribution of the populace over the country.
10. Free education for all children in public schools. Abolition of children's factory labour in its present form. Combination of education with industrial production, &c, &c.

The Republican Party is not much to be admired. It has a pronounced proclivity to serve Big Business, true Capitalism's other enemy, rather than free markets.

Yet it is clear which political party's national platform is consistently closer to embodying the Ten Commandments of *The Communist Manifesto*.

It is also clear whose elected officials and leading current presidential aspirants are calling for things like a steeper income tax, a higher estate tax, taxes on capital and stock transfers, and more federal power over credit. But Capitalism is not inherently partisan. It is as appealing and available to Democrats as it is to Republicans.

As I, Ralph Benko, have written in *The Transpartisan Review*:

> *Jude Wanniski, an editorial writer for The Wall Street Journal and the most outspoken public advocate for Supply-Side economics, was a self-proclaimed Marxian.*

The Supply-side's political quarterback, Jack Kemp, was a former labor leader as was its premier wide receiver, Ronald Reagan. The man who primarily propelled the reduction of the top marginal income tax rate (already down from 70%) from 50% to 28% was ... US Senator Bill Bradley. He did so in partnership with Democratic center-left leader Democratic Representative Richard Gephardt.

Thus, Ronald Reagan's greatest tax-rate cutting triumph got more of its impetus from the left than the right, resulting in a Senate victory margin of 98-2. This is how transformation happens.

On the day Reagan declared for the presidency in 1979 the Dow was at 814. By adhering to the low-tax-rate, stable dollar, policy mix propelled it to well over 20,000. As my colleague Peter Ferrara observed in Forbes.com:

"During this seven-year recovery, the economy grew by almost one-third, the equivalent of adding the entire economy of West Germany, the third-largest in the world at the time, to the U.S. economy. In 1984 alone real economic growth boomed by 6.8%, the highest in 50 years. Nearly 20 million new jobs were created during the recovery, increasing U.S. civilian employment by almost 20%. Unemployment fell to 5.3% by 1989."

Transformation can happen again.

THE CAPITALIST TEN COMMANDMENTS

The Capitalist Manifesto calls for the adoption of these ten commandments of true Capitalism instead of those found in *The Communist Manifesto*:

1. The highest marginal income tax rates for individuals and businesses shall not exceed 28%.

2. There shall be no reduction or elimination of income tax deductions and credits unless matched dollar for dollar by further reducing tax rates.

3. All assets will be indexed to inflation for the purpose of calculating capital gains.

4. No gift, estate, or inheritance tax shall have a top rate of more than 10% and no such tax shall be imposed on any such transfers of $10 million or less, annually adjusted for inflation.

5. The federal government shall generously fund research and development which are the foundation of the nation's prosperity, skilled jobs and material quality of life.

6. The dollar shall be defined as a fixed weight of gold legally convertible thereunto by any person or entity, foreign and domestic.

7. The Treasury and any other instrumentality of the United States shall not incur any additional bonded liabilities except upon approval by two-thirds of the legislatures of the States.

8. Civil asset forfeiture to the federal, state, or any municipal government is prohibited and criminal and civil fines shall be proportional to both the ability of the adjudicated party to pay these and to the severity of the infraction.

9. No regulation effecting more than $100M in economic activity shall be adopted until enacted by the Congress of the United States and signed by the president.

10. No government shall exercise control over wages or prices, including the pricing of telecommunication services, rent, or imposition of a minimum wage

The fifth commandment is provided courtesy of the Honorable Norman Augustine, Lawgiver, who advised us that numerous studies, including those that won Robert Solow and Paul Romer Nobel Prizes in Economics, demonstrate that as much as 85 percent of the long-term growth in America's economy is attributable to advancements in science and technology.

THE CAPITALIST CREDO: TRANSFORMATION INTO UNIVERSAL OPULENCE

The most iconic tale of Capitalism may be Charles Dickens's *A Christmas Carol*. This short work contains a coded message:

Using Capitalism to unleash prosperity does not involve class struggle. It involves generosity and social empathy.

It is not a tale of confrontation. It is a tale of transformation.

Marx and Engels unleashed more than a century of blood-dimmed tides with their romantic utopian call for class warfare. Communism fomented misery instead of liberation.

So what to do?

Let's take a closer look at what *A Christmas Carol* truly teaches.

Ebenezer Scrooge, the wealthy Capitalist, was the very portrait of miserliness. His employee, Bob Cratchit, was a perfect rank-and- file worker. Cratchit's sickly son, Tiny Tim, presented as a most vulnerable, marginalized, member of society.

Had the tale been formulated to show militant Socialists, or Progressives, having their way Scrooge would be pilloried and his fortune pillaged. When various Communist and Socialist regimes have done exactly that to their wealthy citizens it has ended with misery for all but the Socialist rulers.

That, however, was not Dickens's point. Rather, Scrooge was confronted by apparitions of the Ghosts of Christmas Past, Present, and Yet to Come. These confrontations transformed him.

Scrooge gave Bob Cratchit a big raise in salary and became reconciled to his family as a generous benefactor:

> Some people laughed to see the alteration in him, but he let them laugh, and little heeded them; for he was wise enough to know that nothing ever happened on this globe, for good, at which some people did not have their fill of laughter in the outset; and knowing that such as these would be blind anyway, he thought it quite as well that they should wrinkle up their eyes in grins, as have the malady in less attractive forms. His own heart laughed: and that was quite enough for him.
>
> He had no further intercourse with Spirits, but lived upon the Total Abstinence Principle, ever afterwards; and it was always said of him, that he knew how to keep Christmas well, if any man alive possessed the knowledge. May that be truly said of us, and all of us!

And so, as Tiny Tim observed, God bless Us, Every One!

THE COURAGE TO BE UTOPIAN

The solution to our current political and economic predicament does not lie in the destruction of Capitalism. The future lies in its transformation from a form of cronyism to true Capitalism. The solution calls for the end of Feudalism, any system based on status rather than merit.

While our opponents may parade about and demand "full Communism" we will seriously work daily toward full Capitalism, which alone can produce universal opulence.

What is to be done? Let us again take inspiration from the wisdom of Hayek, that great prophet of liberalism. In his essay cited above Hayek commanded the advocacy of a liberal utopia, founded in truly liberal radicalism:

> Does this mean that freedom is valued only when it is lost, that the world must everywhere go through a dark phase of socialist totalitarianism before the forces of freedom can gather strength anew? It may be so, but I hope it need not be. Yet, so long as the people who over longer periods determine public opinion continue to be attracted by the ideals of Socialism, the trend will continue. If we are to avoid such a development, we must be able to offer a new liberal program which appeals to the imagination. We must make the building of a free society once more an intellectual adventure, a deed of courage.

What we lack is a liberal utopia, a program which seems neither a mere defense of things as they are nor a diluted kind of Socialism, but a truly liberal radicalism which does not spare the susceptibilities of the mighty (including the trade unions), which is not too severely practical, and which does not confine itself to what appears today as politically possible. We need intellectual leaders who are willing to work for an ideal, however small may be the prospects of its early realization. They must be men who are willing to stick to principles and to fight for their full realization, however remote.

...

The main lesson which the true liberal must learn from the success of the socialists is that it was their courage to be utopian which gained them the support of the intellectuals and therefore an influence on public opinion which is daily making possible what only recently seemed utterly remote. Those who have concerned themselves exclusively with what seemed practicable in the existing state of opinion have constantly found that even this had rapidly become politically impossible as the result of changes in a public opinion which they have done nothing to guide — unless we can make the philosophic foundations of a free society once more a living intellectual issue, and its implementation a task which challenges the ingenuity and imagination of our liveliest minds. But if we can regain that belief in the power of ideas which was the mark of liberalism at its best, the battle is not lost.

The battle is not lost, and in fact the odds are strongly in our favor if we but decide to join arm-in-arm to make common cause in defense of, and to advance, the greatest economic system ever known to humanity. Capitalism is the only economic system which anyone honestly can point to and say, "it has made substantive progress toward its seemingly utopian aims."

Arise!

True Capitalism, based on service to humanity and the planet, is the only known way of creating universal opulence. Return the undead corpse of Socialism, based on status, to its box of native soil. Make happen the transformation to true Capitalism.

Arise to build the liberal utopia!

Arise to execute the deed of courage: truly liberal radicalism!

Made in United States
North Haven, CT
22 September 2022

24415946R00052